THE VLOGGER'S HANDBOOK

WRITTEN BY **SHANE BIRLEY**

ILLUSTRATED BY **AUDREY MALO**

QEB

Quarto is the authority on a wide range of topics.

Quarto educates, entertains and enriches the lives of our readers—enthusiasts and lovers of hands-on living.

www.quartoknows.com

Author: Shane Birley
Illustrator: Audrey Malo
Designer: Karen Hood
Editors: Amanda Askew and Emily Pither
Editorial Director: Laura Knowles
Art Director: Susi Martin
Creative Director: Malena Stojic
Publisher: Maxime Boucknooghe

First published in 2019 by QEB Publishing,
an imprint of The Quarto Group.
6 Orchard Road, Suite 100
Lake Forest, CA 92630
T: +1 949 380 7510
F: +1 949 380 7575
www.QuartoKnows.com

A CIP record for this book is available from the Library of Congress.

ISBN 978-0-7112-4287-6   **33614082113563**

Manufactured in Guangdong, China CC072019
9 8 7 6 5 4 3 2 1

Contents

The Art of VLOGGING

Let's

Hey there! Want to learn something about the art of vlogging? You'll be happy to know you are in the right place! You may be wondering where to start, you may have already posted a vlog or two, or maybe you're an experienced vlogger—whatever your situation, this book will give you the tools you need and help you to achieve your full vlogging potential. Who knows—you could be the next A-list vlogger.

So, What's a Vlog?

A vlog is a video form of a blog. Some people also call them "video blogs" or "video podcasts." Wait, but what's a blog? In a nutshell, a blog is an online personal diary. By combining the two words "web" and "log" together, we get the slang phrase "blog." Vlogger is a combination of the words "video" and "blogger."

Vlog!

To be a vlogger, all you need to do is set up a video camera, record yourself talking into the camera, and tell a story. The story could be about something you've experienced, it could be about something you're randomly thinking about, or you could tell your audience about something you have learned. You could talk about cool games, things to do, or even your pets.

Vlogging is an art form. It's an opportunity to be really creative. Vloggers can communicate to an online audience in an engaging way that text or images can't achieve. There are plenty of skills vloggers learn that are technical, such as filming and editing, but once you master them, you can use those skills to create your own unique expression of how you see the world. This book will guide you through the

" *Share your thoughts, ideas, and skills* "

process of creating your own vlogs—from getting inspiration and generating ideas to filming and sharing. You will also meet some real vloggers, who will share their advice and tips for you to apply to your own vlogs.

Let's get on with it. Turn the page to find out more!

Why Do PEOPLE VLOG?

So, why do people decide to record their lives and upload it for all to see? What do they get out of it? For some vloggers, it can be hard for them to explain why they like to document their life and share it with millions of strangers.

Social Connections

The clearest answer is simple: humans are social creatures. We love to hang out with friends and family, and we seek to connect with others. What better way to do that than to tell others about our lives using online video.

Q&As

Throughout this book are question and answer panels featuring successful young vloggers, giving their personal tips and stories about how they got started. Check the Q&As for some extra inspiration and motivation. Head to page 93 for more information about the vloggers and their vlogs.

Q&A WITH SKYE, "IN REAL LIFE" VLOGGER

Q: WHY DID YOU START VLOGGING?

A: I started vlogging for myself. I wanted to be able to look back when I'm older and see all of the fun and crazy things I did as a teenager! Vlogging is fun and I love creating videos and finding new ways to film and edit them.

Professional Bloggers

There's a rumor out there that vloggers can make a lot of money, and some do. But making vlogging your full-time career takes a lot of time, effort, and patience. For most professional vloggers, it takes years for them to make it their full-time job and not all of them are successful.

Why Do YOU WANT TO VLOG?

Now, pause for a moment and ask yourself why you want to vlog. Are you looking for fame? Are you looking for a place to voice your thoughts and opinions? Do you want to film something funny and share it with the world? Let's break down your ideas and see what bubbles to the surface.

Ten Reasons Why

On a piece of scrap paper or a sticky note, write down one reason why you think you want to vlog. Write the first thought that pops into your mind and don't take too much time. Place your piece of paper on the floor or stick it to the wall, then repeat that with your next reason until you think of ten ideas. The important thing here is you want to be able to see all of your reasons in one place. This might also help you work out what kind of vlog you want to do.

Ask for Help

Another tip is to ask your parents or friends to help. They might be a great source for helping you to come up with reasons for why you should vlog. Vlogging may seem like a one-person job, but it doesn't have to be.

Vlog TYPES

Many vloggers follow a specific style or type of vlog. Having a clear style can help vloggers establish an identity and attract followers. Looking at different formats might help you to generate your reasons for vlogging and you might find some inspiration about the type of vlogger you want to be. Let's have a look at some popular vlog types:

Product Reviews

These are videos where the host shares their opinions about a product or service. For example, you could review a new toy, a new pair of sneakers, or new flavors of a food product. What do you think of the product? Would you recommend that other people try it? Giving the product a rating can be a good thing to include in your reviews.

Gaming Vlogs

Recording yourself while playing a video game is incredibly popular. This style of vlogging can take a bit more time to set up as it requires more technical expertise to run, but there are thousands of video channels online that share game play with audiences everywhere.

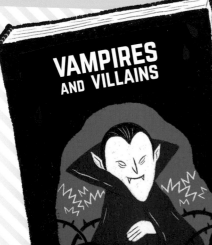

Readers and Reviewers

Some book lovers like to record reviews and share opinions of the books they have read. There are a huge number of book vloggers talking about books, discussing tips on how to write, and reviewing the latest bestsellers.

"In Real Life" Vlogs

Many vloggers start their video hobby by turning on a camera and seeing what happens. Vloggers share some details about their day and simply chat to the camera. It is one of the more popular styles and is worth experimenting with.

Beauty and Fashion

Some vloggers like to show their audiences how to put on make-up or inform them how to choose products that are ethically made. If you like to experiment with makeup or talk about the latest style of clothing, you could record a series that shows people how to create the best outfit or makeup techniques ever.

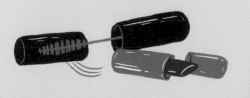

Travel Vlogs

Many vloggers document their travels around the world and share them with other adventure seekers. You don't have to be a globetrotter to be a travel vlogger, though— you could vlog about your family holidays, school trips, or even your journeys to school!

How-to Videos

Are you someone who likes to be helpful? Do you want to teach people a cool new skill that you already have? You could talk about how to be a good skateboarder, how to draw, or how to decorate cakes. Maybe designing your vlog around your natural talent is a great way to boost your vlogging prowess.

Popular Culture

There are plenty of channels out there dedicated to talking about the latest superhero movie or the latest animated film. Running a channel about films, graphic novels, or television programs is sure to gain a following.

Comedy Sketches

Do you like to perform for your family and friends? There are a lot of vlogging channels that focus on making people laugh. Why not try to write a script and film it to see what happens.

INVENT YOUR OWN STYLE

Some of these vlog types are more popular than others, but don't let that stop you—they aren't the only types you can create. Sometimes it's easier to follow an established format, but you might find that it limits your creativity. Playing with form, audio, and visuals may be the best path to your greatest vlogging videos. Play and have fun—who knows, you may end up inventing a brand-new style for others to follow.

Try It OUT

But wait, vlogging can be a lot of work! Have you ever recorded yourself on camera? Have you tried talking to a camera just for fun? If you haven't, don't feel scared or overwhelmed—give it a try!

Just Hit Record

Are you feeling like you have nothing to say? Do you feel like you don't know enough to talk about a particular subject? If you can't think of what to say or if you haven't planned out your vlogging episode (we'll get to that later) try this one simple trick:

> *"Try hitting the record button to see what happens."*

Many vloggers, podcasters, and bloggers find that if they just hit the record button and start talking, magic can happen. It can force your mind to pick a topic to chat about and you might be surprised at what you will find. There are so many stories and ideas floating just beneath the surface, it takes a simple splash to start a small wave of creativity. If you give your stories a place to go, they might just burst out and help you build a vlogging episode.

Remember that there's no need to actually upload a video until you're ready to—this trick is all about getting the creative juices flowing and testing out some ideas, even if the results are terrible!

Generating IDEAS

Think,

This chapter is going to give you some tips on how to come up with great vlog ideas. Don't stop at just one idea. Let out all of your ideas—there are no silly thoughts. To get your creative juices flowing, here are some handy suggestions to help you to become an idea machine.

Sixty Second Challenge
On a blank piece of paper, write down as many ideas as you can in one minute. Take a look at your ideas and see which stick in your mind.

Doodle
Drawing your vlog ideas can help you to come up with subjects you may like to talk about on camera.

Build a Question Tree
If you are trying to generate ideas, you might have a lot of questions. Writing them down will help you to find answers to those questions.

Go to a Park
Put on your shoes, head outside, and let your mind wander. Take a deep breath and speak your thoughts about your vlog out loud.

Write, Invent

What Would "So-and-So" Do?

If you get stuck forming ideas for your vlog, try a little role play. Put yourself in the shoes of another person or character. Ask yourself questions like: "what would my little sister do?" or "what might my favorite celebrity say?"

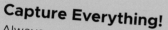

Capture Everything!

Always carry a notebook with you or write your ideas in a note on your phone. Be ready to record even the smallest ideas so that you can read and review them later.

Find Inspiration

Are there any other vloggers that you admire? Write a list of what you like and don't like, and what you have found interesting to watch in the past, to inspire you.

When in Doubt, Read

Allow yourself to get caught up in a book and let your mind digest the text. This can provide you with the mental fuel that your mind needs to develop new ideas.

Developing IDEAS

Once you've generated a list of ideas for your vlog, it's time to pick one and take it further. You can save everything you don't choose for later episodes, but first you need to pick a topic to get you started.

I Choose You!

Some ideas will seem like they are very exciting and filled with creative action, whereas others might seem interesting but not terribly fun to make. The trick is to just pick one! You could spend a long time sorting through every idea you have, but until you start filming, you will never know what there is to discover!

Q: HOW DO YOU COME UP WITH IDEAS FOR YOUR VLOG?

A: I have a lot of interests and I tend to have a "jack-of-all-trades" type of channel. So, I often look at what my last few videos were and see if there are things I haven't done in a while. If it's been a while since I made a ukulele cover, or made a vlog updating my audience on how my writing is going, I might think about doing one of those videos as my next one.

Take it Further

To help you turn an idea into a filmed product, try writing three bullet points that you want to talk about and just film yourself talking about them. The hardest part about getting any vlog off the ground is developing what it should look and sound like. You may repeat this process a dozen times before you say to yourself:

> "*This is what I want to do.*"

You need time to rehearse and experiment—it won't be perfect the first time! It could take you several tries to find your voice and work out what you like best.

Q&A WITH ALEXANDRA, MUSIC AND CULTURE VLOGGER

Q: WHAT ADVICE DO YOU HAVE FOR CHOOSING THE BEST IDEAS TO VLOG ABOUT?

A: What are your interests? Do you have a skill you want to get better at, like playing an instrument, or dancing, or making sculptures? Do you have a lot of opinions on movies, tv shows, or video games? Do your friends tell you that you are good at telling funny stories about your life? Always decide what to vlog based on what YOU want to do, not what seems to be "popular." You'll have a lot more fun, and you'll like the end product more!

Q: ONCE YOU'VE PICKED A TOPIC FOR AN EPISODE, WHAT DO YOU DO NEXT?

A: I would figure out when in my schedule I have time to film and edit, and what I need to get (supplies, lights, props, etc.) in order to be ready to film a take as soon as I turn the camera on!

Planning Your
FIRST VLOG

Here are some ideas to help you plan your first vlog before you start filming for real.

Location

Will the topic you want to cover work better outside or inside? For example, if you want to talk about ice skating, maybe record it while you are skating on ice! If you want to be outside, then scout some possible locations and take pictures of them. If you want to shoot something indoors, why not build your own film set. This could mean dressing up a corner of your room or simply setting up a table and chair.

Super Script

The next step is to write a simple script. It can be exactly what you intend to say or some bullet points that you will talk about on camera. Remember, we're only planning right now, and we'll get into a lot more detail later on in the book.

Q: DO YOU WRITE OUT A SCRIPT FOR EVERY EPISODE OR DO YOU LIKE TO IMPROVISE?

A: For my first ever video, I had a script ready as I was new to it all, although as the camera started to roll, I began to improvise. Nowadays, it depends on the type of video I'm filming. If it's a big video, for example, I will follow a script to avoid rambling, as this can result in a lengthy video.

Q: HOW DO YOU PICK AND CHOOSE YOUR CLIPS?

A: I tend to use all of my clips, although each video will be edited during the editing process.

Q: DO YOU HAVE A PLANNING PROCESS THAT YOU REGULARLY USE TO CREATE A VLOG?

A: It depends on the type of video I'm filming; if it's a big video that would need lots of planning, for example, a fashion look book, I'll carefully plan the layout of the video, outfits that will be worn, the angles that will be used, and lastly, the camera that I'll be shooting with. If it's a simple sit-down vlog, I usually improvise.

Q: WHAT INSPIRES YOU TO CONTINUE VLOGGING?

A: My supporters, which may sound a little cliché, but the support I receive from my videos is absolutely heart-warming. I get viewers from across the globe and it's honestly mind-blowing. Getting messages from my supporters telling me that my videos made their day, makes my whole week, which makes vlogging worthwhile.

Online SAFETY

To Share

It may sound like some of the excitement is being taken away, but it is important to think about your online security before you start posting videos online. There are a host of things that you can do to make your time in the vlogosphere safe and manageable.

Nothing is Forgotten

The first thing to understand before you post your first video is everything you upload will be on the Internet forever. The Internet has a great memory and even if you post something on the web and then choose to remove it, a computer somewhere has kept a copy. Computers don't always do this on purpose and most of the time they are just trying to be helpful.

FAMILY AND FRIENDS

There are many times when relatives of famous vloggers are identified, but it is vital that you think about the privacy of your family and friends—and talk to them about it first. As a responsible vlogger, you must respect other people's boundaries when you are actively filming. Not everyone will want to have their face recorded and uploaded to the Internet.

or Not to Share?

METADATA

Did you know there is a lot of hidden data contained within video and photo files? This information is called metadata and it can reveal details about you. Metadata stores information such as the date and time, the type of camera used, the size and dimensions of the video or photograph, and the camera's location.

GEOTAGS

A geotag is an electronic tag that assigns a geographical location to a photograph, video, or a social media post. Geotagging information can therefore let people know where you live. It's important to remember this when you are editing your video or making thumbnails so you avoid sharing geotags with your audience.

Most video editing software will give you the option to remove metadata and geotags when you create the final version of your edited video.

What Secrets SHOULD YOU KEEP?

Vlogging is all about sharing information, but there are some pieces of information that you should keep secret. Here are some tips that you should keep in mind before you click upload.

Why Not Send Me an Email?

To avoid sharing your personal contact details with the world, it's a good idea to set up a separate vlogger email account. Once you start promoting an email account to your vlogging audience, they might want to send you messages and you might receive spam. Keeping your personal email account private means your inbox will be tidy and maintains a good level of separation between your vlogging and personal life.

Addresses and Landmarks

You may choose to film your vlogs at home but be aware of what you are filming. Watch out for including anything that shows off your home address or any obvious landmarks. You don't want viewers to know exactly where you live! If you spot anything after filming, you can edit things out, use blurring, or even cover things with cute emoticons. We'll look at these techniques in the editing section on pages 60–71. If you review your footage and decide you can't cut or cover landmarks appropriately, maybe film the vlog episode a second time.

If your vlog has a name like The Pug Vlog you could use "thepugvlog@example.com"

You've Got Mail!

It is not uncommon for vloggers to receive physical mail from their viewers—there are plenty of vloggers who film themselves opening fan mail. It is a great idea to get a PO Box address to share with your viewers. A PO Box is actually a "post office" box, usually found at your local post office. You will need to check it from time to time but it keeps your home address out of the limelight.

Did you know Santa Claus has a PO Box for the North Pole? You can write to him all year long at: Santa Claus, North Pole, H0H0H0, Canada

Happy Birthday!

Hiding your birthday can feel like you're concealing the best secret in the world, but to keep your personal details safe, it's best not to tell the Internet. Don't give your audience your exact date of birth and keep references to it vague or choose not to talk about it at all.

If you really want to celebrate your birthday online, consider changing it to another time of the year and celebrating TWICE!

Using a
PSEUDONYM

Have you ever thought about having a secret identity just like a superhero? When you start vlogging, you might want to use a fake name or a pseudonym. Many bloggers do this to protect their real identity. You might contemplate using a different last name, try on your middle name for size, or invent an entirely new name.

Use Your Subject

Let's say for a moment that you want to vlog everything about baseball. You make plans to talk about your favorite baseball teams, how they're doing in the league, and you want to share detailed player statistics. Something you might have some fun with is to list all the words you can think of to do with baseball and combine them to make up a new name for your vlogging persona. Names such as Homerun Larry, Vlogger on Deck, or Barry Up are examples of using a subject well.

Do You Speak Another Language?

Another tactic for inventing a new name can be using words from a different language. If you speak more than one language, you should be able to discover a gold mine of name combinations! Choose from several real-world languages or even make use of fictional languages from books and movies. By combining several languages together, you can make a unique identity for your vlog.

GET CREATIVE

Whichever method you use, remember the key is to protect your personal information. But that doesn't mean you can't have fun inventing your online self. Get creative and see if you can come up with a catchy new identity. But pick one *before* you start creating your online accounts because you should use it wherever you share your vlog.

SEARCH FOR YOURSELF

One of the drawbacks to having a public persona is that people will want to talk about you and it may be a good idea to keep track of what people are saying. Searching for information about yourself can feel a little strange but keeping track of what your audience is doing can also help you generate new videos in the future.

Things you might find on the Internet about you: other vloggers mentioning your vlog, articles, reviews, drawings, poems, and fanfiction.

Password
PROTECTION

One of the downsides of becoming a successful vlogger is you can become a hacker's target. Some vloggers have had their accounts compromised, their videos deleted, and their online channels removed. It is so important to prevent others from accessing your accounts by having secure passwords and adjusting the privacy settings on your Internet accounts. Here are the main things you need to do to keep your accounts secure.

The most secure method for locking your devices is a pin code (a series of up to six to eight numbers), but more modern devices can also do facial recognition, patterns, or fingerprints.

LOCK YOUR DEVICES

Many vloggers use their mobile devices to film their vlogs and if you want to do the same thing, you need to be careful. For example, if you forget your device at school, anyone who picks up your phone could potentially post your videos and images online. But you can protect yourself, even if you drop or lose your device. Every laptop, tablet, and phone has the ability to securely lock every time the screen turns off.

What's the Password?

Having a great hard-to-guess password is an absolute must as it will make your online life more secure. Here are some simple tips that you should do to keep your passwords safe.

* Create your passwords using a combination of random letters, numbers, and special characters (exclamation marks, question marks, percent signs, underscores, etc).
* Never use the same password for all of your online profiles. It might make it easier for you to log into your accounts, but it will also make it easy for someone who guesses your password as they are likely to try the same password on every account.
* Don't ever use a plain dictionary word, the name of your cat or dog, or even your birthday. Simple words and simple word combinations are very easy to crack especially when hackers use special software to hack accounts.

"#WSOYBIFODFOB! Sounds cool!"

I'LL BE YOUR PASSWORD MANAGER TODAY

Password managers help you to create, remember, and secure your password list. Companies such as Google and LastPass (one of the most popular available) offer free services for vloggers and computer users. They also have great advice on how you can use their software to share your passwords between your laptop, tablet, and phone.

INTRODUCING MULTI-FACTOR AUTHENTICATION

One of the most secure ways to lock your account from evildoers is to use Multi-Factor Authentication. The most common way to set this up is to connect your mobile phone to your online accounts. Then whenever you (or someone else) log into your account, it will send your mobile phone a text message. In the text message will be a series of numbers, a random list of letters, or a short password that you must type into the security verification screen either on your laptop or desktop. This confirms that you are real and not a hacker.

You should set up this type of verification on all social media accounts, not just your vlog.

Ask an Adult

If you're ever unsure about your online safety, or if you see anything that looks suspicious, ask an adult for help and guidance. If your account has been compromised, it's often easier to fix the sooner you act.

"Protecting Twitter, Facebook, Instagram, and any future social platforms is a wise move."

SECURITY CAN BE FUN

It might seem like a big deal and it might be annoying at first, but you will have a better vlogging experience when you know your videos are protected. Try making a game of it. Create a list of difficult passwords and then see if you can memorize them. Perhaps you can make passwords that are incredibly long sentences that only you will remember. Adding a little bit of fun is important and will make all of this security stuff easier.

"They'll never guess this!"

EQUIPMENT

The

You don't need lots of expensive gear—you may even have a lot of it in your house already. There are a few key items that you'll need, though, including something to film your vlog! Here are some suggestions to help you consider what tools you need to start filming.

Camera

Your camera is the most important piece of your vlogging equipment. There are many types to choose from and you should pick your camera based upon what you want your vlog to be. If you film your vlog in your bedroom or in your garden, you can use a fairly generic camera. But, if you want to be more adventurous, like diving out of airplanes or swimming underwater, you'll need to consider a more compact camera with special abilities.

Mobile Device

If you are lucky enough to have either a smartphone or tablet, you may already have everything you need. Most smartphones can record video and audio, and some might even have features for editing video. Using your phone might not be the best quality for a vlog, but it can be the quickest way to get started.

Lights

Many vloggers use lighting to keep their vlogs bright and in focus. You might even be able to use lights you already have, such as reading lamps and desk lamps, or film in a bright room.

Tools You'll Need

Tripod

A tripod is a stand that you can use to position and keep your camera still, to stop your video from looking blurry. But not all vlogs need a tripod. Instead, you could set your camera on a stack of books or on a nearby table. Keeping your camera level and your face in-frame is the goal. If you decide your vlog is walking and talking, you might benefit from having a tripod. You can attach your camera and use the tripod as a handle similar to a selfie-stick.

IT DOESN'T NEED TO BE NOW

Any vlogger will tell you that cameras, lights, and microphones can be a hefty investment. But don't let a lack of lights or a low-quality camera stop you from starting your vlog! You can always save up money to purchase your dream equipment or you can arrange to borrow video gear. If you don't know anyone with the stuff you need, libraries sometimes allow you to borrow cameras and lights. Some libraries also have recording booths and video editing software.

Microphone

Most cameras come with a built-in microphone. The usefulness of these microphones can vary and the audio quality will depend on where you are and what type of background noise may be around. If you shoot your vlog outside, everyday sounds can overwhelm your microphone and drown out your voice. The only solution for poor audio quality is plugging in an external microphone.

Editing Software

To clean up and make changes to your vlogging episodes, you will need editing software. Luckily for the beginner vlogger, most computers include editing packages for video. These pieces of software can be quite basic but they usually have enough features to make your videos look good. If the software you have turns out to be terrible, don't fret, there are plenty of free options out there for both video and audio.

ACCESSIBILITY

When you shoot and edit your video, you should take a moment to consider those who may have an issue with their hearing or eyesight. There is a growing need for vloggers to include viewers unable to appreciate everything recorded. When you are editing, there are some things you can do to keep your content as accessible as possible.

Using Transcriptions

For vlog watchers unable to hear, transcriptions are important. Transcriptions are small amounts of text that are displayed on your video at the correct moment so that people who have hearing difficulties can follow what is being said. Transcriptions also allow you to indicate loud noises, when music is playing, or why you may not be speaking at that moment. Transcriptions can be time-intensive and take some practice to put together. However, some video platforms include computer-generated transcriptions and give you the ability to edit them. If you write scripts for your vlogs, you could use those as transcription notes.

"What would your audience need to see and hear?"

> *"Transcriptions are also useful for viewers who want to watch content silently or without headphones."*

Be Descriptive

For those viewers who have problems seeing your vlogs, it can be helpful for you to clarify what is going on in your video from time to time. Illustrating what is being shown or providing some details about the scene can be worked into your dialogue with the camera. For example, if you are outside and walking through the woods, you could describe the environment as you move through it. With enough practice, this can be quite simple to do.

Get Started with
YOUR STORY

By now, you must be eager to start filming your first vlog. You've written a script and jotted down your main bullet points for your first episode. Now it's on to the next step—filming.

The Three Acts

To start filming your vlog, you need to know what story you want to tell. Most stories have a logical beginning, middle, and ending. Thinking in three acts will give you ideas about how to film each setup, conflict, and resolution.

(1)

SETUP

Firstly, you need to introduce the episode. Tell your audience what's going on and why you're talking to them today. Remember, many vloggers use a similar opening style for all of their vlogs.

Example: To tell a story about walking your dog, sit down, press record, and say: "Today, I decided to take my dog for a walk."

"Three acts... let me think..."

Filming Your Vlog

2

CONFLICT

You need to work out what the conflict or problem is that you're trying to solve during the vlog. This will make your vlog more interesting and entertaining both for you and your viewers.

Example: Perhaps when you leave your house, it is pouring rain and your dog doesn't want to go outside.

3

RESOLUTION

You are looking for a solution to the conflict that you've set up. Make sure your story is focused on coming to an ending that satisfies you and your viewers. Don't quit in the middle of your story!

Example: You solve the problem and end your vlog by putting a raincoat on your dog and giving him a tasty treat to convince him to come outside with you.

Visual
STORYTELLING

Film is a visual medium. The first moving pictures did not have any sound—everything needed to make sense visually without any words. Use the power of visual storytelling to help your vlogs be compelling.

Show, Don't Tell

Make a list of shots that you need to visually tell a story, such as how you wake up in the morning.

You will be telling a whole story without saying a word.

Shot 1: get out of bed

Shot 2: walk downstairs

Shot 3: pour a glass of orange juice, make and eat your cereal

Tips

* Get to the point! Don't talk for a long time without finding a setup, conflict, and resolution.
* Go slow! Take your time and explain your thoughts carefully. Don't talk too quickly or dump all of your thoughts at once.

Visual Transitions

To keep your story moving forward, use visual transitions. Once you start editing your video, use shots of your set or environment to change from one part of your story to the next. So whatever the content of your vlog is going to be, film a few different things in every location to allow yourself some editing wiggle room.

Shot 4: go upstairs

Shot 5: brush your teeth and wash your face

Shot 6: smile in the mirror, you're ready to go!

TYPES OF VISUAL TRANSITIONS

* **B-Roll:** Extra shots of your location that can help you create great vlogs.
* **Special Effects:** If you or someone you know is interested in special effects, these can be fun to explore.
* **Drones:** These flying machines can shoot really interesting footage.
* **Time Lapses:** Set up a camera and let it run for a long time to help establish the feel of a location or to transition from one scene to another.

Camera
PLACEMENT

There are three main options for you when filming your vlog. You can have a stationary camera, an operated camera, or a user-operated camera.

Stationary Camera

Called locking off a shot, the camera stays still in one place (though you and others can move around). The benefit of this approach is that a stationary camera helps the audience focus on you. However, it's good to remember that you are limited in terms of how much you can move around because the camera is not following you.

Operated Camera

Someone else operates the camera and can move around in a space or even change location while you vlog. Using this technique allows for greater flexibility but you will need someone else available to help you out. Also be aware that some people are better at operating cameras than others!

Q&A WITH SKYE, "IN REAL LIFE" VLOGGER

Q: WHERE DO YOU NORMALLY PLACE YOUR CAMERA?

A: If I'm making a sit-down video, I mount it on my ring light in the center of my room and anywhere else, I either hold it or set it on any eye level surface I can find.

User-operated Camera

Often called "walking and talking," many vloggers choose to carry their cameras around with them wherever they go. Using this technique, they talk to their camera while they are doing some other activity. It can be effective when you want to show something exciting or if you are traveling from one place to another. However, it can be distracting to your audience if your camera bounces around.

The Rule of Thirds

Using the rule of thirds makes your vlog more interesting for viewers. Look through your camera and draw imaginary lines dividing what you see into thirds. The lines go from left to right and from top to bottom, giving you nine squares. Your focus shouldn't be right in the middle of the frame, but always slightly to one side.

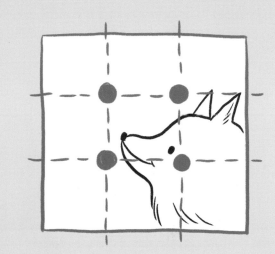

Q: WHAT CAMERA ACCESSORIES DO YOU FEEL ARE THE MOST IMPORTANT TO HAVE?

A: If you're going to be making lots of sit-down videos, then the most important thing is a ring light or other types of good lighting. For vlogging, the most important thing is a camera case and a neck strap for your camera! Also, a flip screen is very helpful for any type of video.

Q: DO YOU MOVE YOUR CAMERA AROUND WHEN YOU FILM?

A: Yes, I do this in most of my videos. If you have a good camera, it should be fine, although if you're filming with a mobile phone, it could get pretty shaky. I think on-the-move vlogs are really good because they keep viewers on the edge of their seat.

Set and
LOCATION

To make your vlog look great, you need to understand some basics of visual composition. If you take a bit of time to create a set, it can help to make your vlog interesting to your viewers.

Your Focus

Before you start filming, think about your focus and the three key areas in your shot:

FOREGROUND

This is you, always as the main focus. You might be talking about and showing your latest book purchase. You won't really move out of the foreground.

Q: WHERE DO YOU VLOG?

A: I tend to film in my bedroom because I have a lighting setup in there. If I film outside, I'll do it somewhere interesting. For example, downtown where there's a lot going on, or out in nature with tons of beautiful sights.

Q: WHAT CHALLENGES HAVE YOU FACED WHEN FILMING ON LOCATION?

A: Bad weather can destroy plans while filming—I always check the weather before I leave the house.

Q: HOW DO YOU DECORATE YOUR SET?

A: I love adding little trinkets that reflect my interests. I have a passion for travel, so I have a globe and an old camera on my set.

BACKGROUND

This is the area farthest away from the camera. It tends to be a wall or a larger piece of furniture. Make sure your backgrounds are clean and interesting, and even colorful. You don't want your visitors to be distracted by a pile of laundry or a messy table of homework.

MIDDLE GROUND

This is the space immediately behind you. Here, you might have smaller "set pieces" such as a chair or a small bookshelf. You want to have something that enhances your subject.

Where Are You?

To get started, create an establishing shot and show the place where you are filming. You don't need to tell your viewers where you live, but just give an idea of where you are. For example, if you are in a cookie factory, film the factory doors as you go inside. Or if you are sitting on a diving board, film your feet dangling above the water of the pool.

Be Inspired

Wherever you decide to film your vlog, it's an opportunity to explore the environment around you. Locations can even inspire you to take your vlog in different directions. Sitting by your fireplace might mean you're having a relaxed chat with your viewers...but what types of locations might allow you to take your audience on a fun adventure? There are lots of possibilities!

Props

Using props can help jazz up your set and set the scene of your vlog. Make sure you plan what you need before you start filming and have everything on hand. Practice doing some test shots to see how the props look on screen before you start filming for real.

Sharing IT LIVE

In recent years, live streaming has become popular with vloggers. It is where you record your vlog and broadcast it over the Internet in real time. There are a few benefits from the usual record-and-post method that we have been talking about.

Audience Feedback

Streaming platforms provide tools so you and your audience can interact with each other. Some streaming systems let the audience send comments and emojis to you as the broadcaster. This gives you a sense of how your audience feel about what you are broadcasting.

Live Discussion

A different feature of streaming platforms is live chatting. When you live stream, your audience can talk to you at the same time. Most often the people watching can also have discussions with each other. They can ask you questions, make comments to others, and also make requests.

Scheduling

There is a potential drawback to live streams: your audience needs to be present for the streams to be successful. Streaming platforms don't keep your video streams live forever. However, you can download your video, edit it, and upload it to your usual vlogging platform.

Sharing Your Screen

If you do live streaming from your computer, it's possible to share the screen with your viewers so they can see what you are looking at. For example, many popular live streamers share videos of themselves playing video games in real time. Their audiences enjoy watching the game play. They can comment on the action and give the player tips on how to solve puzzles so the gamer moves ahead.

* Live streaming requires more technical expertise as it's more difficult to set up and needs a powerful computer.
* You'll want to be organized and prepared in advance. You cannot easily stop the camera once you've started to make a second try.
* Remember to turn off your live stream camera when you have finished!
* Live streaming can be done on the go from a mobile device, but make sure you have enough data available.

Lights, Lights, ACTION

When you think about lighting your vlog, what do you picture in your mind? Do you see an intimate setting with only a single light source, or do you imagine a number of lights like on a movie set? Or maybe you see yourself simply being outside, lit by the sun?

Why light your vlog?

Lights help to establish mood and bring an artistic element to your episodes, but the main reason for using lights is to keep your camera in focus.

The Lights You Need

You don't need expensive lights for a great-looking vlog, but the lighting you choose will depend on what type of vlog you want to film. Also, you may not need the same lighting for every vlog you make. Review the space where you will be filming. Is there natural light or will it need additional lighting? With your vlog script in hand, record some test shots and review them in your editing software. Ask yourself, "Is this what I want?" If not, try again with a different lighting setup.

Lighting Your Vlog

Types of Lighting

There are a few different types of lighting and each can be used in different ways. Try out more than one to see which works best. You might even decide to use more than one, but try to keep your style consistent.

SIMPLE ARTIFICIAL LIGHTING

Indoors, try using a simple light, such as a desk lamp. Think about where the lamp should be positioned—behind, to the side or front of your face, or farther back, lighting up the whole area.

PROFESSIONAL ARTIFICIAL LIGHTING

We'll look at this in more detail on pages 46–47, but once your vlog becomes more established, you may want to invest in professional lighting. Mastering these lights will allow you to shoot at night time without anyone realizing!

NATURAL OUTDOOR LIGHTING

If it's a nice, bright day, why not try filming outside. Again, beware of directly facing yourself or the camera at the sun. But the shade of a tree on a sunny day would create a happy mood. Don't forget to think about what you'll do on rainy or wintery days.

NATURAL INDOOR LIGHTING

During the day, sit in a room with a big window. Beware of the sun shining in your face, so you end up squinting, or shining straight at the camera.

Natural LIGHTING

Most vloggers use simple lighting sources and setups. The easiest way to light your vlog is to use natural light—it's free and it can make your vlogs look awesome! Many vloggers use it almost exclusively.

What is Natural Lighting?

The sun supplies natural light. Nothing beats filming in a bright room where the light is almost perfect from every direction. It provides flexibility and choice. If you don't like a background, turn the camera's direction and shoot against a different one. Easy!

How to Get Started

If you watch other vlogs, you might think they look like a television program or a movie. But it's best to start simple. Take a look around your home and see what types of lights are available to you. Then, go outside and look at various locations to see sunlight and shadow. Feel free to change your location and try different times of day. Seek out unique places where the light inspires you.

Benefits

* It's free.
* Your shooting space can be totally flexible. Reviewing a local park? Done. Want to sit in a café and talk to your watchers? Not a problem.
* If you want to vlog whenever you feel like it, without any preparation, natural light is perfect.
* Good natural lighting isn't harsh on your face, so you'll look just like you're sitting in the room with your viewers.
* If you're out and about, you'll draw less attention to yourself if you have minimal gear.

Q&A WITH ROWAN, TRAVEL VLOGGER

Q: WHY DO YOU USE NATURAL LIGHT?

A: Natural light can create a certain feeling that artificial light can't mimic easily. The golden hues of light in the morning can help create some beautiful shots.

Drawbacks

* You need to shoot all of your vlogs during daytime.
* You can't control the weather, so using natural lighting can be unpredictable and sometimes unreliable.
* Bright sunshine can be difficult to work in, creating dark, unattractive shadows or causing you to screw up your face.
* Rainy, dark, dull days will give you darker videos than you may want.

REMEMBER

Remember to keep yourself out of direct sunlight. It might seem like a good idea to light yourself this way, but cameras don't like the brightest light in the sky. Try sitting where the light is diffused and reflected around—perhaps under a tree or in the shade of a building.

Q: HOW DO YOU DEAL WITH LIGHTING PROBLEMS?

A: Shadows can be tricky when you're filming. I avoid wearing baseball caps in my videos because they can leave shadows on my face.

Q: WHAT IS YOUR FAVORITE TIME OF DAY TO SHOOT YOUR VLOG?

A: Filming at dusk and at dawn can provide very good lighting, however, if you're filming inside in a room with windows, night is the best time. At night I have complete control of my lighting without the sun's interference.

Artificial LIGHTING

If you're after a more specific look, or if you can't film vlogs during the day, you'll need lights. There are a lot of choices, from basic desk lamps to computer-controlled lights. What you use will depend on how much you can afford and what you truly need.

Umbrella Lights

You have probably seen this type of light on photo days at school. It looks like a large umbrella with a bright light mounted inside. Many photographers use this kind of light because it is portable and provides a decent level of brightness. They are perfect for beginner vloggers because they are both compact and fairly inexpensive.

Ring Lights

Ring lights are a circle of lights that surround a camera's lens. They come in various sizes and are mounted either on, directly in front of, or behind your camera or mobile device. It provides a well-rounded solution for vloggers who spend a lot of time talking directly into the camera and are not that far away. However, the light can feel overly bright or hard on your subject and you may need to experiment with the distance between your face and the light itself.

Box Lights

If your vlog needs more than a single source lighting your face, take a look at box lighting. These large reflective boxes contain one or more high-powered lights, which are usually mounted on a tripod. Each box is a bit bulky, but it makes the light softer on camera. You can fill more of your set with this style of lighting and sit a bit farther away from the camera.

LED Panels

Flat panels of LED lights are new to the vlogger world, but they are popular because they're compact, and LED bulbs last a long time. As a bonus, they also change color and brightness.

Benefits

* You have 100% control over the lighting.
* Your setting and time of day are both totally flexible.
* You can create some really cool effects.

Drawbacks

* It can be expensive.
* You may need to carry a lot of heavy gear around with you.
* Preparation will be essential for every shoot.

Q: WHAT'S THE BEST ARTIFICIAL LIGHTING SETUP THAT YOU'VE USED?

A: I bought two basic soft box lights online. I generally set them both up at a diagonal to me, so neither of them are glaring right into my eyes, and they're a fairly equal distance apart from each other. Occasionally, to get a softer light that is still brighter than the dimness of my room, I'll point one or both of the soft boxes at my ceiling instead of at me and it diffuses the light through the room and just generally brightens everything slightly.

Q: WHAT TYPES OF LIGHTS DO YOU RECOMMEND?

A: Soft box lighting is the best that I've used. You can buy basic sets online, and they are fairly easy to set up yourself and move! But honestly, I think natural light is good enough for most things.

Q: DOES SOMEONE ELSE HELP YOU WITH YOUR LIGHTING?

A: Nope. It's just me!

Your Lighting
SETUP

Regardless of what lights or configuration you choose, you will need to know how to set them up. If you have only one lamp, your setup is as simple as turning on the light, making sure you are in focus, and hitting the record button. However, if you need more than one light, here's the best method for lighting your scene.

Tips and Tricks

* Spend time practicing with complicated lighting setups. If you experiment with having more than one light, you could find yourself using too many lights when a single light would do.
* Avoid overexposing your shots (too much light) and making everything look white with little or no detail.
* Watch out for underexposing your vlog (too little light). Your footage will look gray, washed out, and have little depth.

Using the Three Point Method

When shooting video that needs artificial lighting, the secret trick is that you only need three.

1. **The Key Light** is the most powerful of the lights you will use. It is the brightest and will light your face at an angle. Pick your best side and turn on the light.

2. **The Fill Light** is positioned at an angle on the opposite side of your key light and should be about half as bright. It removes or lessens the shadows caused by your key light.

3. **The Back Light** is pointed at the wall behind you or at the back of your head. This kind of light creates depth by putting space between you and your background.

Back light

Key light

Fill light

Color
MAGIC

One of the cooler ways to experiment with lights is to use color. Why? How? Let's find out!

What's in a Color?

Colors can suggest a tone to a vlog before you even speak. Many filmmakers use color to set the scene of their films and suggest emotions that their viewers should feel while watching.

How to Add Color

There are many ways to add color to your videos. Here are just a few:

* Hang colored fabrics over a lamp.
* Pick up some colored bulbs for an easy way to inject and swap colors.
* Point white light at a painted wall to achieve a subtle tone in your video.
* Also called color filters, color gels are transparent colored materials that you can place in front of a light in the path of a beam.

Just be careful not to put anything flammable on your lights because a "fire-like" glow from a real fire isn't what any vlogger wants!

Mood Board

You can pick any color you want, but here are a few ideas about the mood and tone colors can help create. Remember that different cultures can interpret the same color in different ways —so think of your audience when you use color!

RED

If you want your audience to feel excited, try different levels of reds. The color red can also mean power or anger.

PINK

The color pink suggests innocence and can be playful!

ORANGE

Orange is a good color for presenting happiness and warmth.

YELLOW

Yellow could help give your videos a feeling of hopefulness and joy.

GREEN

Why not try using green to present nature? Darker shades of green can evoke a sense of mystery or spookiness.

BLUE

If you want your video to feel calm, use some different shades of blue.

PURPLE

Historically, purple is the color of royalty and luxury. Just like blue, light shades of purple can evoke a sense of tranquility.

NO COLOR

By choosing to remove color and having your video in black, white, and shades of gray, you can create a sense of the video being very serious or even ominous.

Yo, AUDIO!

How Does It Sound?

Sound isn't just about your audience clearly understanding what you're saying. You can play with sound and create different moods by using the audio track of your video editor. You can do voiceovers, create sound effects, and even add music!

How Do You Record Audio?

Most cameras have a built-in microphone, but it will probably pick up unwanted noises from your environment. For you to sound your best, an external microphone for your camera could be a good choice. Once you plug in another microphone, the built-in microphone should turn off. Test this by recording some video and playing it back.

"Make sure you position the external microphone out of the shot—no one needs to see it!"

Your Audio SETUP

Whichever microphone you use, you will need to set it up properly to get the best audio—of both sounds you want to include (your voice) and sounds you don't want to pick up (wind or noisy traffic).

Microphone Placement

Place an external microphone in front of or beside your camera to record your voice clearly. You may need to experiment a bit to find the best location for great sound!

Make it Visible

In bad weather, a television reporter will usually use a handheld microphone, so their voice can be heard. Having the microphone visible is a practical choice to produce the best possible audio recording and it's also a visual reminder of the act of recording.

Soundproofing for Better Sound

All locations sound different. If you go outside and record with a microphone, it will be quite unlike recording with the same microphone inside your living room. The microphone's recording quality is affected by its surroundings. Many recording studios use soundproofing materials to reduce echoes and you can use this idea to help. Look for space without flat surfaces (or cover those surfaces with blankets to dampen the sound).

Types of
MICROPHONE

To have more control over your sound, take a look at alternative recording options. If you're just starting out, it's best not to spend lots of money until you see whether you need to.

Your Mobile Device Earbuds

When using your phone as a recording device, the earbuds act like a lavalier microphone (see page 55). Some vloggers hide the microphone from the camera by clipping it inside their clothes. It isn't a perfect setup but it's a good, low-cost starting place.

Handheld Microphones

All your favorite singers use these stage microphones, as does your head teacher when addressing the students. Also called condenser microphones, they are designed to be held close to the mouth and only pick up the sound immediately in front of them, so they are ideal for recording human voices. Plus, they're practically unbreakable!

Lavalier Microphones

Unlike handheld microphones, lavalier microphones are hands-free and small enough to clip onto your clothing. You might see these on television when journalists are interviewing people, usually for a longer period of time. Lavalier microphones make it easier to move around or even dance!

Portable Recorder

If you want a flexible option, consider a portable recorder. These expensive microphones don't necessarily need to be connected to your camera and can record the audio track separately. As they are highly sensitive, they often pick up background noises so you'll need to practice to get the best results.

Shotgun Microphone

Attached to the top of a camera, a shotgun microphone is shaped like a long cylinder and points toward the audio source. Filmmakers often use these microphones to get better sound when they record action scenes. They have a protective foam cover or windsock to stop wind noise. You can even hold it really close to the sound to get the best recording possible.

Mixing AUDIO

To review your recorded vlog for what it sounds like, close your eyes and hit play. Like what you hear? If your answer is no, don't worry! Here are just a few ways to improve your audio after it's been recorded.

Recording Audio Afterward

When you start editing your video, you may realize that the audio you recorded is not great quality. To fix this problem, you could return to where you recorded the original video and record a fresh soundtrack, or simply re-record at home. Then add the new audio to your video during the editing phase.

Adding Music

Like any good television drama or movie, background music can set the mood of your vlogging episode better than a few simple words. It can allow you to enhance the mood of your videos and increase your audience's appreciation of your content. Audio has a powerful way of connecting your audience to you.

Adding Sound Effects

As your editing skills get better, you might find yourself wanting to add special sound cues or effects. Sometimes additional sound cues will help your viewers understand what's going on. But don't overdo it—you don't want to distract or confuse your audience.

"Make sure you control the volume of any audio you add, so it isn't so loud that it drowns your voice or so quiet that you can't clearly tell what is playing."

Creating Mood with Music

Here are some ideas for music and sound effects that you could experiment with. Just remember that sometimes less is more!

SCARY
If you are shooting a Halloween video, try adding some creepy orchestra music with sound effects of creaking doors, clanging chains, or screaming.

SAD
If what you want to talk about is a sad topic, add some mellow or slow music to enhance the experience of your audience. You probably won't need sound effects as you want to be taken seriously.

HAPPY
Up-tempo music that makes the listener feel cheerful and uplifted is the best choice. If it makes you smile, it'll probably make your viewers feel the same.

EXCITING
If you're reviewing something exciting, such as a high-speed race or your skiing trip, try some fast-paced music to match the thrill of the action on camera.

UNDERSTANDING COPYRIGHT

Adding music to your vlogs can be fun. But beware, most popular music is under copyright protection—it belongs to someone else and you must obtain permission or a license to use it. Without the right to use a song, your vlog may be banned from a video platform or the rights holder may request payment.

YOUR OPTIONS

CONTACT THE SONG'S OWNER
Email the owner or the company that manages the musician. Remember that very famous people will be busy, so you may need to find a different route to use their music.

STOCK MUSIC LIBRARIES
You will pay a small charge to use music, but they usually hold popular tracks that you may be interested in. The amount you pay depends on how much of a song you use and where you plan to use it. For example, using music on a tv program or ad is much more expensive than on a vlog.

ROYALTY-FREE LIBRARY
Search databases of royalty-free music, which is available at no charge.

PUBLIC DOMAIN MUSIC
Anyone can freely use music in the public domain without asking for permission!

RECORD YOUR OWN MUSIC
If you can play an instrument, sing, or use composition software, you could write and record your own music! It can be a tall order but there are plenty of vloggers out there who do just that!

Q&A WITH FATMA, FASHION, COMEDY, AND LIFESTYLE VLOGGER

Q. HOW DO YOU RECORD AUDIO FOR YOUR VLOG?

A. I use an external microphone which I plug into my camera for better sound quality.

Q. DO YOU USE MUSIC? IF YES, WHERE DO YOU GET IT FROM?

A. Yes, I tend to use a range of songs. Sometimes I use YouTube's copyright-free soundtrack or I reach out to upcoming artists to use their music in exchange for exposure.

Q. DO YOU ADD AUDIO EFFECTS TO YOUR VLOG EPISODES?

A. Yes! I love sound effects and so do the viewers. Silly sound effects can make videos much funnier.

Post-
PRODUCTION

You may decide that your video is perfect just as you filmed it. However, you might want to consider post-production, as cutting and editing can make your vlogs a better experience for your viewers.

Ramp It Up

To help viewers understand your story, you may want to include an introduction and a conclusion, which are sometimes called "on ramps" or "off ramps." As you put together your vlogging episodes, you could use an opening title and ending sequence to make people aware of your vlogging style or keep a consistent look and feel.

"On Ramp"

MY VLOG

"My BMX challenge"

Cutting and Editing

What If Your Story Needs A Little Help?

It's possible that your story would benefit from additional visual material. You may find that you want to show something in your vlog that you didn't or couldn't film. When that happens, you can look online for additional resources (video, sounds, or images) to add to your vlog. There are plenty of free public domain resources available.

Telling Your Story

Some vloggers can get lost when trying to edit their videos. When all the pieces are in front of you, it becomes harder to decide what story you want to tell because you now may have a lot of options. Think about your original plan—if it was good, then stick to it. Follow your instincts about what you think your audience will best respond to.

"Off Ramp"

"Thanks for watching!"

TOP TIP

When editing, think about other vloggers you have watched and how they have edited their episodes. All the choices you make should help your vlog feel more like one you want to see.

Video Editing
SOFTWARE

If you decide to do some post-production work on your filming, you'll need to learn how to use video editing software. It's best to start simply before trying to mimic the most experienced vloggers.

Software You Might Already Have

If you have a computer of your own, the first thing to do is check it for editing software. This software will probably be basic in the tools it offers, but is a great starting point, and the skills you learn can be transferred to any editing software you use in the future.

Minimal Editing via Phone or Tablet

Mobile phones and tablets often have built-in video editing capabilities. However, these are usually simplified versions that may not give you vastly different results. You can choose to install more feature-rich applications, but always experiment with a few programs before settling on one that fits your needs.

Editing on an Apple via Apple iMovie

Apple's operating system contains a program called iMovie. It allows you to edit your video clips together to make a vlog. There are templates and themes to try, as well as soundtracks, to practice what makes your vlog look good.

Editing on a PC via Microsoft Photos

Microsoft Windows 10 contains a program called Photos. Despite its misleading name, it is a basic video editor. Once you open Photos, create a new video project where you put your video clips and photos into a linear storyboard timeline. There are handy themes that can help you quickly put your video together.

Open Source Solutions

If you don't have any programs on your computer, there is software available on the Internet that you can download and use for free. Open source programs are created and maintained by people who volunteer their time and expertise to make great software. Some links to open source solutions are included at the end of this book on page 91.

Some links to open source solutions are included at the end of this book on page 91.

Q&A WITH ALEXANDRA, MUSIC AND CULTURE VLOGGER

Q: WHAT'S THE BEST VIDEO EDITING SOFTWARE THAT YOU'VE USED?

A: I've only used iMovie so far, as I can't afford more expensive programs at the moment.

Q. WHAT SOFTWARE IS BEST FOR A BEGINNER?

A: I'd say iMovie is really good for beginners! It's straightforward, but as you get more comfortable, you can learn how to do more interesting things with the program.

Q: HOW LONG DID IT TAKE YOU TO BECOME COMFORTABLE DOING VIDEO EDITING?

A: I'd done it a couple of times as a teenager in school before I started doing it on my own, and with that, I picked it up pretty fast! Video editing itself isn't that difficult, but finding your own style definitely is.

The Basics of
EDITING

Editing video is fairly straightforward once you understand how editing programs use video clips, images, and audio tracks. These programs treat your media as small bite-sized chunks that can be cut up, rearranged, layered, and then exported as a final video.

A Physical Process

Originally, video editing was a physical process. A projector played strips of film onto a screen, making the pictures appear to move. To edit shots into longer sequences, editors physically cut the strips of film and put them into a different order by taping the pieces together. Editors would spend hours, even days or weeks assembling a rough cut of a film.

Moving Pictures

Films were originally called moving pictures. The first short films were made of only one shot from a stationary camera, which was enough for audiences who were simply entranced with the novelty of movement on film. Over time, filmmaking pioneers began to experiment with telling stories through multiple shots and editing those shots together into a longer film.

Digital Video Editing

Nowadays, video editing still involves cutting and pasting, but by digitally adding and subtracting small video clips until your finished video looks the way you want it to. Using digital software, you can also choose to include clips of individual images or clips of audio.

"Now check out the Director's Cut!"

DIGITAL IS BETTER BECAUSE YOU CAN...

* Load up and review your initial video footage as a series of clips.
* Add more video clips, photo clips, or audio clips.
* Make changes to the order of the clips.
* Use transitions and add special effects.
* Make multiple editions or versions, such as a director's cut or a blooper reel that will make everyone laugh!

TIMELINE TIPS

Every digital video editor will provide you with a clip timeline. It's a handy tool because you can drag your video clips into the timeline to arrange them into your chosen order. It's usually displayed at the bottom of the editor and represents time from left to right with the start of the video on the left.

Editing a Story from Beginning to End

When you add clips to your timeline, remember that you are telling a story from start to finish. Your viewers will expect a logical progression of events, so don't try to be clever and jump back and forth in time unless absolutely necessary. If you play with time, record an additional audio or video piece to explain what is going on.

An Example of Order

The first clip should be followed by a clip that is further ahead in time. For example, think about what you would show in a vlog about your family having dinner together.

Clip 1: Your sister sets the table.
Clip 2: Your parent is cooking in the kitchen.
Clip 3: Everyone sits down to eat.
Clip 4: You all share stories about your day. One of you may even tell a joke that makes the others laugh.
Clip 5: You and your brother grumpily do the washing up.

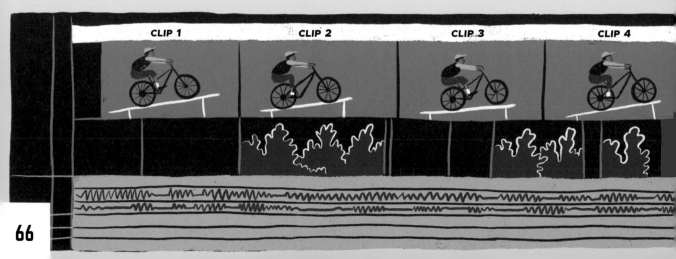

CLIP 1   CLIP 2   CLIP 3   CLIP 4

Q: HOW DO YOU DECIDE WHICH CLIPS GO FIRST?

A: A great thing to remember is that people get bored, fast. A good thing to do is always put a hook clip in the beginning of your video, either about something that will happen later in the video, a surprise for your fans, or a giveaway at the end, etc. Make it a mystery, so they want to watch to see what happens!

Q. DO YOU PLAN YOUR EDITS ON PAPER BEFORE YOU START?

A: I don't plan out video edits on paper, but sometimes I do for video thumbnails! A thumbnail is very important for a video. It usually is a deciding factor for people to click on your video or not, so it is a good thing to plan it out and make sure it's perfect.

Q: WHAT'S THE BEST THING YOU'VE LEARNED ABOUT EDITING?

A: When saving your video from your software to your desktop, make sure all of the settings are set to the highest quality and to compress at best quality.

Thinking in Layers

Layers run from top to bottom of your screen and are usually called tracks. When you look at your timeline, you'll see a number of tracks available. It basically means that two video clips will play at the same time, one on top of the other. For example, you may have filmed a clip of the night sky and want to add an explosion to tell the story of an alien invasion. To do this, you add the night sky clip into the first track and the explosion clip into the second track. When you play the video, you will see the night sky, then the explosion over the top of the sky.

CLIP 5

My BMX Challenge

TRICK A

Track 1

Choosing
YOUR CUTS

As the vlog editor, you choose where to start and stop your video clips. There are several types of commonly used cuts in video storytelling—just remember to always move your story forward.

Standard Cuts (Basic)

Your video clips follow one after the other without any jumps in time, simply telling the story as it unfolds in real time. You might use standard cuts to trim extra footage or arrange shots in a specific order to tell the story.

Jump Cuts (Basic)

When you advance through the timeline, the video clips jump from one piece of footage to another. Usually this jump is only a few moments, but it could even be a few minutes to a few hours forward in time. For example, you could cut from your bedroom to your bathroom or from eating breakfast in the morning to coming home from school at the end of the day.

Cutaway (Basic)

A cutaway shot allows you to show secondary action or other parts of your environment as part of the continuous video sequence. For example, you might pretend to have a conversation with another person in your vlog—but you play both parts! You show this by simply cutting between both pieces of footage.

Montage (Advanced)

This style cuts rapidly between clips to move the story forward in time quickly. You might use this to compress a vlog on how to bake cookies. In about 15 seconds, you could show yourself mixing ingredients, rolling out the dough, putting cookies on a baking tray, popping them in the oven—and then trying the finished treat!

L-cuts and J-cuts (Advanced)

This style of cutting means the audio and video tracks of your video don't match on purpose. An L-cut cuts to a new video clip visually while the audio from the previous clip finishes (which looks like an L-shape in the editing program). For example, if you filmed a plane taking off, you could include audio of you saying goodbye to your parents while the plane rises in the sky. A J-cut cuts to a new audio clip while the previous video images continue (which looks like a J-shape). For example, if your video shows someone dancing outside on a sunny day, you could cut to the sound of thunder while the dancing continues.

How to
ADD AUDIO

In digital video editing software, you can treat audio separately. Even if you recorded your video and audio together, you can break them apart to fix any sound issues.

Cleaning Up Audio

You can export the audio track from your video editor in order to clean it up or make changes. For example, you may review a birthday party clip and hear someone talking when you think silence would work better. Within your video editing software, you can mute that section or cut that snippet of the audio from the video entirely. To be more advanced, export your audio and edit it in an audio specific editing program. Then import it back into your video editor with the changes you want.

Audio Levels

Audio levels are important with any video you edit. You want to keep them consistent and not hurt the eardrums of your viewers—would you want to listen to it? You can adjust your audio levels (either in your video editor or an audio editor) to reasonable levels. Such attention to detail will improve your vlogs.

EDIT   MY BMX CHALLENGE

Practice Different Methods

The best way to learn what works best is to practice by filming a few test shots to cut and edit.

Make three versions with:
1. Only the sounds you recorded.
2. No sound except an audio voiceover.
3. A combination of the recorded sound and voiceover together.

Which do you like best?

Vlogging PLATFORMS

Once you're happy with your edited vlog episode, there are a lot of platforms available for hosting and sharing your work. Some are best-suited for long-length vlogs, some for live streaming, and some for short-length vlogs. You may even want to use more than one platform to reach a wider audience.

Setting Up Your Vlog

If you're ready to jump in and play around with a video platform, why not set up a YouTube account. Like most online services, all you need is an email address, a password, and a name. To create your account, head to YouTube.com and click on the sign-in button. Once your information has been accepted, you can then use this account to sign in to YouTube.

TOP TIP

To keep it simple, pick one platform as your main vlogging platform and share only special episodes on other video sharing services.

WEBSITE HOSTS

WordPress.com, Blogger.com, and Tumblr.com are platforms that you can use to share your content. There are pros and cons for each but they all do a good job at making your vlog accessible. Each has their own design engines and you can find plenty of website templates to change the look of your vlog.

Going Online

How to upload

The specifics of uploading depend on which platform you choose. See page 76 for some platforms to try, and follow the instructions on the platform to start uploading your videos. Remember that if your video files are large, you might need to be patient and wait for them to complete uploading.

Your Own Website

It can be a good idea to have a website. It will allow you to direct people to one location where they can learn about you and the types of content you create. For example, if you live stream videos on one platform and post a regularly edited video on another platform, your website will be able to show both, making it easy for your audience to view whatever they like.

Just Use Social

Another option is to just use a suitable social network to begin with. You could always wait for an audience before setting up a website if you think it would hold you back at the start of your vlogging adventure.

Uploading....

The Basics of
SOCIAL MEDIA

The next task is helping people to locate your video channel. With a bit of planning and experimentation, you can find an audience who will enjoy the vlogs you produce.

The Power of Social Media

Social media offers you a way to share text, photos, audio, and video, all relating to your life. These platforms are places where you can chat with others, view parts of their lives, and make new friends. It is really quite extraordinary because you can virtually meet with people from around the world.

Set Up Vlog Social Profiles

Although you can use personal things about your life, it's a good idea for the social profiles relating to your vlog to have the same name. Then viewers can easily recognize the connection and your social profiles are easy to find.

Sharing is Caring

Of course, the first thing to do is to share links to your vlog episodes. Give people a taste of what an episode will be about and why your viewers might enjoy watching it. Take another look at how the vloggers you admire promote and talk about their episodes.

REMEMBER!

The people you interact with on social media are still strangers. You should always speak to an adult before giving away any details about your real name, phone number, or address, or before any meet-ups are arranged.

Participation is Key

The real trick to making social media work for your vlog is **not** to just talk about yourself and your vlog! Instead you need to take an interest in what other vloggers and people are doing in their lives. Try starting conversations by asking questions, join in with discussions, follow what other vloggers are talking about, and share other vlogs and ideas. You can connect with people in surprising ways if you take the time to listen and respond. It can be a great place to get new ideas for your vlog as well!

Which Social Media SHOULD YOU USE?

So social media can be a good way to share your videos, but which platforms will work best for you? Here are a few ideas about what some of the most popular platforms can offer:

Email Still Works

Newsletters are a great way to keep people informed about your vlog and new episodes. Using online platforms, you can allow people to sign up to your newsletter, and design and send emails as often as you need to. Just remember that by law, you may only email people who have signed up to receive these notifications.

Twitter

On Twitter, it's easy to follow other people and subscribe to their tweets, conduct searches of topics, and post your own thoughts. If you have something to say, you can let people know what you think. But remember to not just talk about your vlog in every conversation!

Q&A WITH FATMA, FASHION, COMEDY, AND LIFESTYLE VLOGGER

Q: WHICH SOCIAL NETWORKS DO YOU RECOMMEND?

A: I recommend Instagram, Snapchat, and Twitter, as these three social networks are very popular in society today.

Facebook

Facebook offers lots of options for a beginner vlogger. It has photos, videos, and live streaming all in one place! You can share pretty much anything you want and people can comment and interact with you easily. You can also create a Facebook Page to help build a community around your vlog. Posting your vlog to your Facebook Page can be an awesome way to let others share your videos with their friends.

Instagram

Instagram became popular because people wanted a simple way to share their photos with others. It features video and live streaming options, so you can showcase your vlog by posting short clips or highlights from your episodes. You could even post video stories talking about why you think someone should watch your latest episode.

"Experiment with different social media platforms—you never know where a potential audience may be hiding."

Q: HOW DO YOU MANAGE NEGATIVE COMMENTS?

A: I tend to block trolls who leave negative comments, that way it prevents me from internalizing their negativity.

Q: DO YOU TAKE ANY BREAKS FROM SOCIAL MEDIA?

A: Sometimes! I'm a student, so I often take some breaks from social media to completely focus on my studies.

Hello HASHTAGS!

#ilovemypet

First introduced on Twitter, hashtags allow you to link your social posts to a theme or word. You can use common words or create hashtags that are unique to you. Hashtags are powerful and very useful for seeking new content or episodes.

How to Use Hashtags

Let's say that your latest vlog is about how you harvested honey from your garden beehive. Using hashtags such as #honey, #bees, and #beehive will provide important keywords and context for your video. Using the same hashtags in the video description of your vlog and on any of the social media platforms you use will also be a key ingredient for searchability. Now if someone searches for #honey, they will find your post and vlogs.

How Many Hashtags?

Some platforms have character limits, but as a general rule, use as many as is appropriate. However, it's important to be sensible... because hashtags also give a sense of context when someone reads a post. Fifty hashtags will be too many for people to look at, so will be a waste of your time.

Trending

When something is trending, it is a popular subject being discussed online on platforms such as Twitter. Trending topics often link to news, politics, celebrities, and the entertainment industry, other current and world issues, and even everyday things.

#ilovemypet

Hashtag Inspiration

Hashtag inspiration comes from all sorts of places. Some hashtags are made-up words, some have to do with events, some are national days, and some are just plain silly. Take a look at other vloggers for inspiration. Here are a few simple ones to get you started:

#vlog
#vlogs
#vlogging
#vloggin
#vlogger
#vloggers
#vloglife
#vloggerlife
#vlogpost
#blog
#blogs
#blogging
#bloggin
#blogger
#bloggers
#bloglife
#bloggerlife
#blogpost
#youtube
#youtuber
#follow

Make Up Your Own Hashtags

You don't have to use popular hashtags —you can use anything you like. The odd hashtag can just be for comedy value.

Hello Hashtags! **79**

Managing YOUR AUDIENCE

Just as you spend time with your real friends, and put in an effort to meet their needs, your audience will become a new friendship group that needs to be well looked after.

Live Streams

You can spend time with your vlogging audience and friends when you host a live vlog. Just turn on your webcam or your camera and talk to your followers. They simply chat back to you while you talk by typing in comments or questions.

What did you think?

☆ ♡   Amazing tricks!

↻ ☺   Wicked moves!

☆

Making Time for Your Audience

The biggest struggle is making time for your audience. If you are a single vlogger, it can be an overwhelming thing to make additional time for people who like your vlogs. Make sure to only add new features for your online world in small chunks. Add your Instagram only if you think your audience would benefit from it and if you will have time to share.

Keeping You Honest

Your audience knows you better than you think. Once they invest their time in watching you, they will offer you the best feedback about what you're doing. Listen to them. Ask them questions about your vlog episodes. Be friendly and know that they sometimes can be a valuable resource in helping you share your vlogs more widely.

Ignore Offensive Feedback

There will always be some people who want to bring you down. They might call you names and they might try to bully you. It is important to remember that you should ignore them! Keep a positive attitude about your vlog and talk to the audience who respects what you're doing.

Skateboard secrets

27 likes

Check out my latest trick!
View all 10 comments

Q: HOW DO YOU ENGAGE WITH YOUR AUDIENCE?

A: I try to answer every comment I get on my channel. I also try to remember as many people's names as I can. When I see someone who's new to the channel, I'll go and check out their channel, watch some of their videos, and leave comments. I try to offer support to others and invite other channels to collaborate in my videos.

Q. DO YOU LIVE STREAM TO CONNECT WITH FOLLOWERS?

A: I have tried to live stream but need more practice. It's a work in progress! My audience likes when I live stream.

Q: HOW MUCH TIME DO YOU SPEND INTERACTING WITH YOUR AUDIENCE?

A: I spend about 30 minutes a day interacting with my audience.

Scheduling
IS CRITICAL

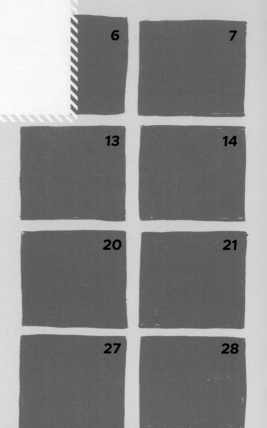

6	7
13	14
20	21
27	28

Ten years ago, television programs were only aired on a fixed schedule and viewers would wait for the next episode. Nowadays, with streaming, we are used to having programs, films, and even vlogs at our fingertips—and new content all the time.

How Much Time Does It Really Take?

Just like a television episode, it can take a long time to brainstorm, shoot, and edit your vlogs. You need to consider how much time it will take to create each episode into a finished vlog. This will allow you to look at your calendar and write in when you plan, shoot, edit, and release. You'll also need plenty of time to come up with ideas, or it may become difficult to consistently produce vlogs to your set schedule.

EXAMPLE SCHEDULE

If your vlog episode takes a week for you to complete, then you can't release more than one per week. Keep a regular plan for both recording and posting your vlog. Remember, being flexible is okay too.

CALENDAR KEY

PLAN

SHOOT

EDIT

RELEASE

DAY OFF!

FOLLOW-UP ON SOCIAL MEDIA

Don't Forget About Your Life!

You have a life outside of your vlog! Be realistic with your time and don't schedule vlogging work every day. Creating one really good vlog a month and being happy and not stressed is much better than trying to do one a week and getting burned out.

Set a Schedule for Your Audience

Your audience has their own lives. They won't always watch your videos immediately after you post them. Try setting specific days for when your new video content is released or give a teaser a day or two before release to create excitement and prepare your audience for new content.

Working Ahead

One trick that vloggers can use to get as many videos out as possible throughout the year is to record several episodes at one time. You could, for example, spend a full week recording a series of videos, editing them, and then scheduling the time when they are released. You could record one of your Christmas episodes in July and release it in December! Using this technique will allow you to see the bigger picture of your video schedule and you can then film videos to fill in gaps.

Getting MORE VIEWS

You've put in a lot of effort to get to this stage, and you may become frustrated if not many people are watching your vlogs or if your audience isn't growing as you expected. There are plenty of things you can do to improve how a potential audience can find your vlog.

Metadata

Writing good metadata is critical to the success of your vlog because it helps both search engines and individuals find your content. Metadata is all under your control and includes the title and description, tags and categories, and image tags.

Pay Attention to Titles

Always make your vlog titles descriptive, clear, and concise. You want to make sure that anyone scrolling through a list of vlogs or on their social feed will pause and take notice. Pay attention to the keywords you are using. For example, a cute video about your pet kitten and how it likes to play with string could be titled: "Cute Kitten Plays with String." The title quickly tells potential viewers about the story of the video.

Descriptions Matter

Every video needs an amazing description to describe the story of the video in more detail. Keywords are even more important here. Putting together a description full of appropriate keywords will give your vlog a higher chance of being found. Be careful, though: you must use natural language in normal sentences when using keywords, otherwise search engines know you are trying to cheat the searchability system.

Your Style is Different

Some people think vlogging is easy! They might tell you to "just make a viral video" and you will find success. The truth is, videos that become viral are very hard to make. It is unpredictable and no one really knows what videos will become Internet sensations. The best thing you can do is to make your videos your way. Being yourself will make your vlogs unique because there is only one YOU!

Tags and Categories

Tags and categories help to organize your content, especially when you have uploaded and shared dozens of vlogs. Tags are a bit like hashtags, simple words that group your videos together. You can use similar tags for all of your vlogs, or whatever pops into your head! Categories are similar to tags, but there tends to be just a few, such as My Home, My Pets, and Books I Like, that never change. In each category, you'll have multiple tags and playlists.

Vlog with Others

No matter what kind of videos you make, there will always be other vloggers who talk about similar things. Why not send them an email and ask them if they would like to work with you on a video project? Many vloggers like to do collaborations, also known as "collabs," where they film an episode or two and then post their edited vlogs on each other's channels. You can then share them with your audience and they can share you with theirs. It is a good way to find new viewers who might like your style of vlogging.

Sorting Your Videos into Playlists

To help your audience find your videos, some sharing platforms let you organize them into playlists. Playlists are lists of videos that have something in common. Playlists can be a list of videos based on a keyword, a series of videos that talk about a particular theme, or a collection of videos about a trip that you took. Sorting your videos can direct your viewers to videos that you think are important or give them the tools to look through the types of content that you create.

Skateboarding tricks playlist

Gnarly tricks

Incredible pro skateboarding tricks

Best skateboarding tricks

Thumbnails

A thumbnail is a picture that represents what your vlog episode is about before the audience clicks on the play button. Think of your thumbnails as little movie posters for each of your videos. Pick one strong image and make it colorful and appealing. Using a suitable thumbnail can make it clear to anyone scrolling by what the video is all about. Images should also have a short description or a few tag words to allow search engines to "see" what they are showing.

Analytics

Keeping your channel going depends on knowing your audience well. Video sharing platforms help you by tracking all kinds of details called Analytics. This includes where your audience visits from, what devices they watch your videos on, how long they watch each episode for, and on which days at which times. Don't get too bogged down in all the data provided. Instead, ask yourself a question, such as "What time are viewers watching and interacting with my vlog?" and use the analytics to try to answer it.

Best of half-pipe skateboarding

Biggest ollies ever

Amazing flip tricks 2

Ten of the best rail tricks

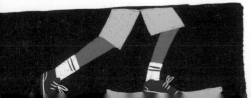

Skateboard tricks that look impossible #3

Freestyle skateboarding

It's a WRAP!

Hopefully after reading this book you'll be ready to record your first vlog or will have picked up some handy tips to help improve the vlogs you've already created. Here are some final tips and tricks to help you love it, live it, vlog it.

Be Authentic

The most popular vloggers aim to be as authentic as possible. They know they must entertain and inspire and they are more successful just by being themselves. If you're feeling happy or sad, make sure you let your audience know. As a new vlogger, you want to be as much of your true self as possible. It's your unique voice that draws your viewers into your vlogs.

Conclusion

Take a Break

As a vlogger, it's important to know when to take a break and to make time for yourself. It can be overly tempting to keep sharing more and more of yourself but establishing rules around what you show on your vlog and what you keep for yourself and your family is an important part of being a vlogger. Remember that you need to find a balance between vlogs and your offline life.

Keep an Open Mind

No matter what you do, keep filming and keep an open mind. Technology is changing all the time and there is always something new to learn—a new camera angle, a new audio trick, or a new way to make your editing workflow faster are all ways that could help improve your episodes.

Useful Links

You'll need reliable tools and resources to help you with your vlogging adventure. Here is a list of links that will point you in the right direction and get your vlogging career off the ground.

Video Platforms

YouTube is currently the most popular service where you can post your vlogs.
www.youtube.com

Vimeo is also a popular place where some vloggers post their content. (May Require Fees)
www.vimeo.com

Tiktok allows you to share 15-second videos (up to 60 seconds if you connect them together).
www.tiktok.com

Facebook lets you share pre-recorded videos on your Facebook Timeline or on a Facebook Page.
www.facebook.com

Instagram offers a quick way to share short 60-second videos.
www.instagram.com

Instagram TV (IGTV) allows you to share longer videos.

Live Streaming

YouTube Live is where live streaming videos exist on YouTube.
www.youtube.com/live

Twitch.tv is a video streaming service targeted at gamers and vloggers.
www.twitch.tv

Periscope allows you to stream video live to the Internet which is deleted 24 hours later.
www.periscope.tv

Facebook Live lets you stream live video from their mobile app. Once you record your stream, your video can be shared on your Facebook Timeline or on a Facebook Page.
www.facebook.com/live

Instagram Live allows you to stream live video through the app but once you stop, the video disappears unless you share it using Instagram Stories.
www.instagram.com

Blogging Platforms

Wordpress is a quick way to create a simple blog and share your video content. There are storage restrictions for file uploads and you may need to pay for storage in the future. www.wordpress.com

Tumblr is a simple platform where you may want to share your vlog. Tumblr does limit the file size you can upload and it only allows five minutes per video per day. www.tumblr.com

Blogger is a popular blogging platform owned by Google. The platform is free and plugs into most other Google services like YouTube and Google Drive. www.blogger.com

Open Source Video Editing

Apple iMovie comes with most Apple computers and has a series of good features. www.apple.com/imovie

Microsoft Video and Photo Editor is a popular video editing suite with simple features. www.support.microsoft.com/en-us/help/4051785/windows-10-create-or-edit-video

OpenShot Video Editor is a well-rounded video editor with a lot of good options. Great for beginners. www.openshot.org

Blender is an open source video editor and 3-D object maker with more advanced features. www.blender.org

Open Source Audio Editing

Audacity is a free, easy-to-use, multi-track audio editor and recorder. www.audacityteam.org

Ardour offers a much more advanced audio editor. www.ardour.org

Photo and Image Editing

The Gimp is an image editing software much like the popular Photoshop. www.gimp.org

Paint.NET is a free photo editor for Windows users. www.getpaint.net

InkScape is a vector drawing program to help you create illustrations. www.inkscape.org

Public Domain Photos, Videos, and Sounds

PixaBay is home to a large collection of public domain photos and video clips. www.pixabay.com

Archive.org is a stock footage library offering a collection of video from throughout history. www.archive.org/details/stock_footage

Vimeo Public Domain Clips includes a collection of video clips that you can use for your vlogs. www.vimeo.com/channels/publicdomain

Pond5 Public Domain Project collects public domain photographs for you use for your thumbnails. www.pond5.com/free

Soundbible is a royalty-free resource for those who would like to add sound effects to their vlogs. www.soundbible.org

Canva is a browser-based graphic design tool. It's a good way to create quick graphics for your vlogs and has handy tutorials to help you along. www.canva.com

Meet the Vloggers!

Feeling inspired by the young vloggers interviewed in this book? If you want to find out more about them, or if you're looking for some inspiration for what to vlog about, why not check out their vlogs and social media?

Alexandra

One small person documenting her journey as she tries to avoid becoming an adult! Check out her videos of song covers, album reviews, creative projects, nerdy escapades, and general life musings.

YouTube: TheVloggingNook
Tumblr: www.thevloggingnook.tumblr.com

Fatma

A fashion, comedy, and lifestyle vlogger trying to make a change. Visit her channel for Q&As, challenges, and how-to videos.

YouTube: ItsFatma
Instagram: itsffatma
Twitter: @itsffatma

Rowan

On his channel, Rowan makes travel and adventure vlogs as well as camera and filmmaking equipment videos.

YouTube: Rowan Elsmore
Instagram: rowanelsmore
Twitter: @Rowan_Elsmore

Skye

A vlogger making videos to help inspire and entertain, hoping for viewers to find and achieve the life they want through her insights. Head to her channel and social media sites for vlogs about all kinds of things, including tips for organization, clothes, and daily life.

YouTube: skyekimi
Instagram: skyehas.nolimit
Website: www.skyekimi.com

Glossary

audience
people who might view a vlog

channel
a central location where vlog posts are uploaded

comments
messages created and saved on a vlog that are visible to other individuals on the Internet

community
audience that supports a vlogger or group of vloggers

copyright
the exclusive right given to the creator of a vlog to publish, sell, or share

editor
a piece of software that provides the ability to create cuts and edits of video footage

followers
people who subscribe to a channel and view your vlog episodes

hashtags
words that show what your vlog or post is about, and group the same content together

keywords
words that show the content of your vlog and are recognized by search engines

live stream
a video broadcast in real time

metadata
small amounts of text that provide detailed information about a vlog episode

platform
a service that a vlogger may use to share their vlog episodes

pseudonym
a false name that is used to identify your personality in a public space

public domain
media that is not protected by copyright and can be used without obtaining permission (as the copyright may have expired or the creator may have chosen to make it free for others to use)

scheduling
the process where you choose and dedicate moments of time to record, edit, and publish your vlog episodes

shot
the moment when the camera starts recording until the moment the camera stops

tags
words added to your vlog episodes used to organize them into groups

thumbnail
an illustration or edited photo that visually indicates the content of the posted vlog episodes

timeline
a visualization of edited video clips to help manage the flow between the video clips

upload
the transfer of a media file from a local computer to an online system

video clip
a shorter piece of a longer video recording used for editing and completing a vlog episode